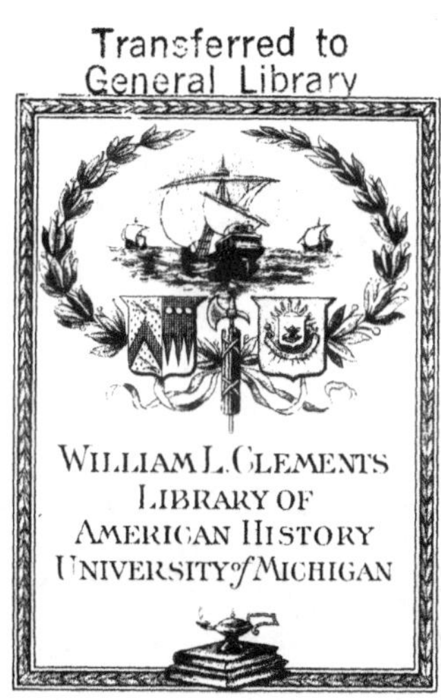
WILLIAM L. CLEMENTS
LIBRARY OF
AMERICAN HISTORY
UNIVERSITY of MICHIGAN

THE UNIVERSITY OF MICHIGAN
·LIBRARIES·
THE UNIVERSITY OF MICHIGAN
ARTES SCIENTIA VERITAS
1817

A
DIPLOMATIC EPISODE.

THE REJECTED TREATY FOR ST. THOMAS.

BY

EDWARD L. PIERCE.

BOSTON:

1889.

A DIPLOMATIC FIASCO.

SOME time ago Scribner's Magazine contained a paper entitled "A Diplomatic Episode," by Miss Olive Risley Seward, which undertakes to narrate the negotiations with Denmark for the purchase of the islands of St. Thomas and St. John in 1866–1869 by Mr. Seward (then Secretary of State), and the connection of the Senate Committee on Foreign Affairs (Mr. Sumner being chairman) with its consideration and failure of ratification. With many words, the introduction of superfluous incidents and assertions of facts not verified by reference to sources, she gives an air of mystery to what was a plain transaction and a very simple question. A map is inserted, as if to produce an optical illusion, on which a number of straight lines converge to St. Thomas as a common centre of islands, continents and commercial marts, just as all roads once led to Rome. Among the statesmen of the time no one except Mr. Seward thought the island worth having at any price, or being taken as a gift for any purpose of peace or war. In a foreign war it would have been useless for offense and difficult of defense; and while, during the civil war, when the Confederates held most of our Southern Atlantic coast, one of the Antilles would have served a purpose as a coaling and supply station, it is no part of national duty to make military preparation for civil war, certainly not a part of ours with the nation consolidated by the abolition of slavery.

Impartial authorities describe St. Thomas as exposed to hurricanes passing once in twenty years over it and doing great damage; with very frequent earthquakes coming with serious shocks at intervals; with often recurring droughts; with no running stream and only one small spring, the only resource for fresh water being the storing of rain; its only present productions "a few vegetables, a little fruit and some guinea grass," insufficient for one-twentieth of its inhabitants; its population "one-tenth white, two-thirds black and the remainder mixed;" its utility for commercial purposes dwindling from year to year, and its imports falling off one-half from 1870 to 1880; abandoned as a rendezvous by the British Mail Company in 1885, with other important lines following its example. From the end of our civil war, during which its trade had a temporary stimulus, its descent in importance has been constant. ["American Cyclopædia," "Encyclopædia Britannica," article "St. Thomas."] This is the prize which Mr. Seward won for us, but which was lost by the mysterious indifference and perversity of all the statesmen of his time! Of St. John little need be said here, as scarcely anything was said of it during the discussion. In extent it is somewhat larger than St. Thomas, but so unattractive and repelling that it was "an almost abandoned island" (C. H. Bithome to Mr. Seward, May 13, 1867). Providence, as if to save us from a wild venture, gave in the midst of the negotiations a triple warning by an earthquake, a tidal wave, and a hurricane, in quick succession.

Ours, too, is a country of the temperate zone, and the aspirations of its people are continental. There has been among us a healthy resistance to going further southward than we have now reached, or seeking islands either in the Atlantic or the Pacific; an instinctive reluctance, as shown in the later case of St. Domingo, to enter on a career of tropical extension, with dangers and embarrassments to free institutions which could not be measured in advance.

It is not difficult, since the recent astounding revelations of Mr. Lincoln's biographers, to comprehend the wildness with which Mr. Seward entered on this extra-territorial scheme. It now appears that he was hardly warm in his seat as Secretary, when, with a civil conflict of tremendous import at hand, he proposed to the President to rush madly into a war with France and Spain, and nominated himself for dictator! The patriot of to-day cannot value too highly the wise instinct of the American people which at Chicago in 1860 preferred Lincoln to Seward. It is now apparent why the good President, though he kept his own counsel, leaned afterwards rather on Mr. Sumner than on his Secretary when foreign questions were pending. The admirers of Mr. Seward have a new task of apology and defense quite enough to exhaust their ingenuity.

The underlying thought of "A Diplomatic Episode" is that the Senate of the United States in withholding assent to Mr. Seward's negotiation put our country in the position of acting in bad faith to Denmark. This contention has no basis in fact, or political ethics. The Constitution of the United States, of which all the world in doing business with us must take notice, confers on the President "power by and with the advice and consent of the Senate to make treaties, provided two-thirds of the Senators present concur." It confines this great power, an incident of sovereignty, to the President and Senate, each acting with an independent responsibility and discretion, neither having the right to abdicate in favor of the other. This discretion of the Senate has been freely exercised in dealing with strong as well as with weak nations; for instance, in the rejection of the Johnson-Clarendon treaty on the one hand, and of the St. Domingo treaty on the other. All publicists are agreed, among our own the authors of the Federalist, as well as Story and Wheaton, that treaties bind neither party in law or in honor, until finally ratified by all the bodies in which the authority is placed by the constitution of the State.

Whence comes this gloss on the Constitution that the treaty-consummating power is now wholly lodged in the Executive, and that the Senate has lost its constitutional right of withholding its advice and consent? If this notion were to prevail some future Secretary, head of a bureau not established by the Constitution, swaying some future Andrew Johnson, might carry our dominion into Mexico, to the Isthmus, to the Amazon, even to Cape Horn, to say nothing of countless islands; and the Senate, representing sixty millions of people, would have to stand aloof in amazement, shorn of all power to arrest the madness! Aside from its merits, the fate of the St. Thomas treaty was of great advantage, in that it established against a monstrous assumption of one-man power the prerogative of the Senate to act on all treaties with absolute freedom of judgment, unhampered by executive initiation and pledges.

The purchase of Alaska from Russia is not analogous to the attempt to acquire St. Thomas. In the one case the territory was continental, in the other extra-continental and insular; in the one case lying to the north, in the other tropical; the one bringing wealth in fisheries and furs and fair climatic conditions, while the other was without resources actual or undeveloped, and even subject to derangements of nature unparalleled within the same limited space ; the one checkmating the colonial empire of Great Britain in the northwest, and opening the way to the dominion of the continent which has been the thought of far-seeing statesmen like Sumner and Cobden, while the other was to bring to us two worthless islands of the size of a county, two of the thousand in the Caribbean Sea, with a waste of money in peace and complications in war. Alaska exceeded half a million square miles and the price was $7,200,000, while the bargain with Denmark called for $7,500,000 for a meagre area of only seventy-five square miles.

It is true that Mr. Sumner added to his main argument for Alaska, made April 9, 1867, the consideration that "the dishonoring of the treaty," as he called it, at that stage would involve a serious responsibility. But he was very careful to confine this *obiter dictum* to the case in hand ; and Miss Seward very deftly, as well as abruptly, cuts short her quotation from his speech when she reaches his emphatic exclusion of all other treaties from any implied sanction. He went on to say that "had the Senate been consulted in advance before the treaty was signed or either power publicly committed, *as is often done on important occasions*,* it (the Senate) would be under less constraint," a clear intimation that this should be the practice in such cases. And then, to make his *caveat* emphatic, he said, "Let me add that, while forbearing objection now, I hope that this treaty may not be drawn into a precedent, at least in the independent manner of its negotiation. I would save to the Senate an important power justly belonging to it ;" and, he added, "this treaty must not be a precedent for a system of indiscriminate and costly annexion." He also expressed his anxiety that our expansion should come from natural processes, without war and *even without purchase*, the latter to be justified only under peculiar circumstances. Mr. Sumner in this *caveat* gave Mr. Seward and the Danish negotiator timely warning as to the determination of the Senate to hold fast to its constitutional prerogative, which they had no excuse not to

* Mr. Seward submitted in 1862, in advance, the draught of a convention with Mexico for the assumption in part of her debt, and, the Senate advising against it, the negotiation went no further.

keep in mind the following October when they made their definite arrangement.

No one knew this constitutional limitation better than General Raasloff, the principal negotiator on the Danish side. He had lived among us almost as a citizen when engaged in engineering enterprises; and he had already represented his country in the United States as Consul General and Minister. He wrote our language without foreign idiom and spoke it almost without foreign accent. He knew our polity as well as we know it ourselves. Indeed, unlike the case of Russia, where the Czar holds the power absolutely and exclusively without hindrance from any one, the Constitution of Denmark contained a limitation analogous to that of our own, making the treaty-consummating power dependent on the decision of the Rigsdag. The treaty was itself explicit, reserving, as conditions, ratification by our Senate and by the Danish Rigsdag, and also by the islanders themselves. Rejection by any one of the three would have involved no breach of faith.

It was natural that the Danish negotiator, whose personal pride as well as whose party interests were at stake, should make the point of good faith; but he labored hard in insisting upon it when pressed before the Committee on Foreign Affairs by Mr. Fessenden's question, "Would, in your opinion, the United States have a right to complain if your Rigsdag had refused their consent to the ratification of the St. Thomas treaty?" His answer was that in that event the Rigsdag would have been dissolved, and a new election ordered; and then, if the new Rigsdag followed the action of its predecessor, the Cabinet itself would have resigned. And this was all the satisfaction he could suggest as possible; clearly none for a nation disappointed in a bargain, and insisting on a point of good faith. He thought, too, that we should still have had the right to complain that his government had trifled with us "in having neglected to secure beforehand the ratification of the treaty,"—an intimation that Mr. Seward should have made himself surer of his footing, and have consulted the Senate in advance, as pointed out to be the proper course by Mr. Sumner in his speech on the Alaska purchase.

Whatever color of justice there may have been in Denmark's point of good faith came from Mr. Seward's unauthorized assurances that the enterprise was sure of approval in the Senate;

and according to the Washington correspondence at the time, the Committee on Foreign Affairs at their hearing January 28, 1869, thought them to be "an egregious blunder" when General Raasloff made them the basis of his appeal. Mr. Seward said to the Danish negotiator, June 28, 1866, that "the Executive could always count upon the assistance of Congress in matters of this kind provided the proceedings had been correct;" and in other communications gave the Danish Government to understand that there need be no fear as to the ratification. Arguments in newspapers and pamphlets at the time put the case for ratification chiefly on the ground that Mr. Seward had committed us to the treaty by his ill-considered and precipitate action. Raasloff's intimate friends laid the blame of his misfortunes on Mr. Seward. Mr. G.V. Fox, writing to Mr. Sumner, January 31, 1869, concerning General Raasloff's appeal for his good offices to assist the treaty, suggested that the Foreign Affairs' Committee invite his opinion, and said, "This course seems to me the only one which enables me to satisfy my friend, General Raasloff, that I have attempted to aid him in the most unpleasant position in which Mr. Seward's diplomacy has placed him. I can see that there is no possibility of success for him, and that the rejection is fatal to his future in his own country." Raasloff himself, writing to Mr. Sumner January 12, 1869, and referring to the effect of the rejection on his own career, speaks of himself as "having been more than anybody else (Mr. Seward, of course, excepted) instrumental in bringing such a calamity and humiliation upon my country." The parenthesis, which is his own, is significant.

The writer of the "Episode" insinuates that prejudice against Seward as well as Johnson accounts for the want of welcome which awaited the St. Thomas treaty in the Senate. It is unnecessary to resort to this theory, for the objections against the treaty would have been equally fatal if it had been negotiated by a Secretary and a President who were retaining the confidence of the country. It is true that Mr. Seward had been "swinging around the circle" with Mr. Johnson. He is understood also to have been the originator of that fatal policy of the President which revived the rebel spirit, disorganized the whole Southern country, led to barbarous legislation against the colored race, eventuated in riots, massacres and Ku-Klux raids, and postponed for a decade the pacification of the restored States; consequences which in charity we must believe he was not wise enough to foresee. He avowed himself openly its supporter, and historical writers declare him to have been its author. The general disfavor into which he fell may have had something to do with producing the popular distrust of the Johnson-Clarendon negotiation; but it does not appear to have affected the convention with Denmark. One thing is certain, that Mr. Sumner at no time prejudged Mr. Seward's diplomatic enterprises; but uniformly came to their consideration with an open mind. They had parted politically, but the spell of an old friendship and common memories was still on Mr. Sumner, probably also on Mr. Seward. Together they had fought the good fight of "the irrepressible conflict." They had long enjoyed intimate fellowship in the Senate, never broken by antagonism or weakened by rivalry. They had sat often at each other's table, and these household recognitions continued to the end of Mr. Seward's service in Washington. Mr. Sumner had been at least once a guest at Auburn, where another than Mr. Seward regarded him with almost motherly affection, addressing him even by his Christian name. There had been full sympathy between them in personal trials and sufferings, and in bereavements, and also when each at different times was prostrated by the assassin. Each had a fascination in manner and spirit which the other felt; and who, with large sympathies with his kind, that has known either has not felt the same? On a day in June, 1860, shortly after his loss of the nomination for President, I dined at Mr. Seward's house in Washington, with Sumner and Adams as the only other guests; and it was difficult to keep back the tears as our host with profound disappointment but in no unmanly way spoke of what had recently passed at Chicago. Between Mr. Seward and Mr. Sumner there were differences in the treatment of public questions, sometimes temporary chafing and soreness, particularly during Mr. Lincoln's administration, when the President gave heed on important questions of foreign policy to the Senator rather than to Mr. Seward, as with reference to the issuing of letters of marque and reprisal, so that the latter said impatiently, "there are too many Secretaries of State." But never was Mr. Sumner inhospitable to Mr. Seward's plans or wishes, even after the contest between Congress and President Johnson had begun. As soon as Mr. Seward had negotiated the treaty for Alaska, a few hours before it was signed, he sent for Mr. Sumner, March 29, 1867, to come to his house the same evening to confer with him and the Russian minister concerning it. With what vigor Mr. Sumner sustained that treaty is a part of history. When shortly after its ratification I asked him how he came to take so much interest in it, and to prepare so laborious a speech in its defense, he stated several reasons of a public nature; but first in order of time he gave Mr. Seward's earnest desire to carry it through.

Mr. Sumner recognized always the duty of co-operating cordially with public officers with whom he might not at the time be in political sympathy. He continued during Johnson's administration to call often at the State Department when Mr. Seward was Secretary, and to keep himself informed as to its business and needs, and in debates, even during the heats of the impeachment controversy, contended so vigorously for Mr. Seward's recommendations as to clerical force and the contingent or secret service fund as to invite the suggestion from some associates that he was too much the partisan of that department. Any one curious in such matters may verify this statement by consulting the Congressional Globe's reports for January 30 and 31, February 4 and 7, and June 22 and 23, 1868.

The "Episode" makes and reiterates against the Senate the charge of delay in acting on the St. Thomas treaty, a charge which lies against the negotiators rather than the Senate. More than three years passed between January 1, 1865, when Mr. Seward opened up the subject of the purchase to General Raasloff at Washington and the time when the treaty and necessary papers were ripe for the consideration of the Senate. The intervening period was occupied with inaction on both sides, principally the Danish; more or less skirmishing between the parties as to the government from which the first offer of amount should come; prolonged silence and inattention of the cabinet at Copenhagen after Mr. Seward's first offer, which our minister at that court was unable to break [Mr. Yeaman's letters to Mr. Seward, January 21, March 13, April 27 and 30, and May 2, 1867]; finally, instead of an acceptance of Mr. Seward's offers one counter proposition and then another; the Danish minister at Washington going home and leaving no successor; the insistence of Denmark after the price had been fixed on a vote of the islanders, which, in view of what they were, could be of no significance, and which involved vexatious questions and postponements, so that the treaty was not signed till October 24, 1867, and not submitted to the Senate till December, and the vote of the islanders was not communicated till January 17, 1868. Although in December, 1867, when the treaty was referred, Mr. Sumner promptly requested the papers from the State Department, they were not forthcoming for seven weeks, and when they had been printed and were available for use, the time fixed by the treaty for ratification, February 24, 1868, had expired, and an extension of time became necessary. So sluggish were the Danes in the whole business that our Minister, Mr. Yeaman, could not control his impatience, and wrote of the national characteristic, "In everything, from cobbler to king, they are the most deliberate and leisurely people in the world." In the purchase of Alaska, on the other hand, between the first broaching by the Russian Minister and the final signature there was less than a six months' interval.

No one saw more clearly than Mr. Seward the peril to which the delay at Copenhagen exposed the treaty. Its only chance of approval in this country grew out of the peculiar exigencies of a *civil* war, when a long southern coast was held by the insurgents, and that period was receding. Military considerations were diminishing in force, and ambition for territory was not the passion of the hour. Every day, too, the administration, of which Mr. Seward was the inspiring leader, was losing the confidence of the country. He telegraphed January 19, 1867, to Mr. Yeaman, "Tell Raasloff, haste important." In a letter to Mr. Yeaman, August 7, 1867, he urged on the Danish government "promptness in the pending negotiation as essential to success;" and in letters September 23 and September 28, a month before the convention was signed, he emphasized the hazard to which the procrastination at Copenhagen had exposed the whole business, as in the meantime the people of the country had lost interest in the acquisition of a naval station in the West Indies and were turning their attention to other and cheaper projects. He wrote: "The desire for the acquisition of foreign territory has sensibly abated. The delays which have attended the negotiation, notwithstanding our urgency, have contributed to still further alleviate the national desire for enlargement of territory. In short, we have already come to value dollars more and dominion less." It was evident that Mr. Seward before the treaty was submitted to the Senate, and even before the convention was signed, had lost faith that it would be ratified, not because of any peculiar adverse influences in that body, but because the American people had become unfriendly to such a purchase. It was a dead treaty when Mr. Seward handed it to the Senate, as he well knew at the time. This appears from his letters to Mr. Yeaman, as well as from his letter to Mr. Sumner, November 9, 1868, when replying to the latter's inquiry as to another matter, he wrote: "It is true on the contrary that instructed by the debates of Congress and the tone of the public press during the past year, I have declined all recent suggestions in regard to the acquisition of naval stations anywhere in the West Indies, especially the mole of St. Nicholas."*

The author of the "Episode" suggests foreign influence at Washington operating against the treaty. This, of which she gives no proof, is the creation of her imagination. When, where, and on whom was it exercised? Was Mr. Seward approached in that way, and does this account for his losing heart in the project? Was Fessenden bought up by some German lobbyist? Did British gold find its way into Cameron's pockets? How were Morton, Patterson, Harlan, Casserly, and Sumner taken care of? One, without recurring to Horace (*Nec deus intersit*, etc.), ought to be wiser than to resort to such an unnatural explanation.

The Danish negotiator in his letters to Mr. Sumner and in his speech at Copenhagen named as his only difficulties "the prevailing ignorance of facts" (which he hoped to remove by proof of the value of the islands as a naval station), and the contest between the President and Congress; but he gave no hint of foreign influence. In fact the only influence of this kind exerted at Washington was in favor of the treaty—through the attractive qualities of General Raasloff whom all wished if possible to serve, and the refined hospitality which he freely dispensed. Besides, he argued his case on two different days before the Committee on Foreign Relations, and did what he could to affect public opinion. He called to his service as counsel to enlighten senators, a gentleman who

*The House resolution against further purchases of territory, passed November 25, 1867, by a vote of 93 to 43, was, as explained by the speeches of its mover, C. C. Washburn, November 25 and December 11, intended as a protest against the purchase of St. Thomas.

combined social favor with professional accomplishments. He employed an able and well-known writer to prepare a pamphlet argument in favor of ratification, and supplied him with documents concerning the treaty which had been printed by the Senate as confidential, and he sent this pamphlet to senators and to the leading journals of the country, in which it was reviewed. Articles in favor of the ratification appeared in Paris contemporaneously in the *Moniteur* and *Pays*, which indicated a prompting from the same source. It is safe to say that a pressure of such various kinds by a foreign power to carry a treaty in the Senate is without precedent.

The paper under consideration seems to attribute to Mr. Sumner altogether the failure of the treaty in the Foreign Affairs Committee, for the reason that he was "almost implicitly followed by it." He had indeed with the committee the weight which comes from a combination of perfect integrity, sound judgment, large experience and technical knowledge; but the other members, Fessenden, Cameron, Harlan, Morton, Patterson and Casserly, were not men naturally of his type, none of them anti-slavery leaders like himself, every one of them at times strongly differing from him. Mr. Fessenden was antipathetic to him, and disposed to be critical of what he did. If Mr. Sumner was unfair, if he did aught unbecoming a Senator, there were sharp eyes to follow him. Mr. Fessenden, it may be remarked, was the member most demonstrative against the St. Thomas treaty, and he was one of the only two Senators who voted against the Alaska purchase. Clearly Mr. Sumner's "over-mastering advocacy" in favor of this last treaty did not influence the Senator from Maine; and the latter's resistance to the St. Thomas project came equally from his independent volition.

There are insinuations in Miss Seward's paper which are unworthy of any kinswoman of the distinguished statesman whose name she bears, and which he, if living, would be the first to rebuke. In three passages, at least, she imputes to Mr. Sumner an unworthy and deceptive silence, and a hypocritical purpose to mislead General Raasloff and give him false hopes of a ratification of the treaty. In all this, as well as in the other charge of "smothering" the treaty ("secretly and silently done," she says), there is no truth. Happily, the amplest record evidence is at hand to disprove them. As many as twenty-five letters or notes from General Raasloff to Mr. Sumner, from December, 1868, to May, 1869, the period during most of which he was at Washington urging the ratification, are preserved, and are in my hands.

The purchase of St. Thomas did not attract Mr. Sumner, but he kept an open mind concerning it, and as far as possible held his judgment in suspense. He had a regard for Denmark as a nation and a particular friendship for Raasloff, and sought to give every opportunity to him to prove the value of the acquisition. He arranged for Raasloff personal interviews with his colleagues, and what was quite exceptional, if not unprecedented, formal audiences with the committee January 26 and January 28, 1869; obtained documents for him which he sought in order to remove objections to the purchase, distributed pamphlet arguments for the treaty among the members of the committee which Raasloff supplied, and intervened at his request to obtain the opinion of Mr. G. V. Fox, which was known to be in favor of the purchase. He was the one member of the committee to whom Raasloff applied freely for good offices, which were uniformly granted. Nevertheless, he was never converted to the treaty. Raasloff's surviving friend, General Christensen, says that he frequently spoke of Mr. Sumner's connection with it, "always regretting that he could not win the sympathy of that statesman for the transaction."

The committee suspended action, but this was in order that Mr. Seward and Raasloff should have the fullest opportunity to complete all proofs and supply all considerations in favor of the purchase. Mr. Seward never called for a decisive vote; and both he and General Raasloff knew that there was no time when the treaty would have been carried; and they thought with diminishing hope that there might be a favorable turn. It was a ratifying vote which they desired, not a vote with the certainty of a rejection. The non-action of the Senate was at Raasloff's express instance, as proved by a contemporaneous record. Mr. Fish wrote to Mr. Sumner, March 28, 1869, a note containing only these words: "Dear Sumner: Raasloff does not wish any action on his treaty. He will probably see you. H. F."

The imputation of sinister silence on Mr. Sumner's part is effectually disproved by General Raasloff's contemporaneous letters. In December, 1868, probably late in the month, he arrived in

Washington with a view to press the treaty. At once he began to send Mr. Sumner notes and letters about the treaty, as well as congratulations on New Year's day and invitations to dine; and they were meeting from day to day. On the evening of January 11, 1869, Mr. Sumner told him frankly that there was little or no chance of his success with the committee and the Senate, and sympathizing with him in the probable effect of his failure on his position at home, said: "I am sorry for you; you are in a tight place, etc.," words which were repeated by Raasloff in a note the next morning, and which he said had kept him awake a good portion of the night. In the same note and in another written a few days later, he said that he was fully prepared for the worst, and had all along been prepared for it. He felt, however, constrained to push his case, and went before the committe on the 26th and 28th of the same month, and otherwise did all he could to save it, but in vain. At the last of March he left Washington, never to return. Just before his departure Mr. Sumner gave him the portrait of Thorwaldsen, which he acknowledged March 28, 1869, saying "it would be very dear to him as a *souvenir d'amitie.*" The gift was made after Mr. Sumner had forewarned Raasloff of the doom of the treaty, and had, neither in the mind of giver or receiver, as Miss Seward sets up, any import of favorable action upon it. Raasloff wrote from Copenhagen May 19, "Let me thank you once more for the beautiful portrait of Thorwaldsen. It is much admired both on account of the historical interest attaching to it, and as a work of art. I hope I may be allowed to keep it." He had gone from our country not to return, but his thought of Mr. Sumner was as affectionate as ever.

An authentic statement of General Raasloff's appreciation of Mr. Sumner's relations with himself and of the Senator's conduct concerning the treaty appeared in the General's speech made at Copenhagen after his return, when all active pressure for the ratification had finally ended. The occasion was a celebration of the amalgamation of some telegraph lines. Writing to Mr. Sumner May 19, 1869, a few days after the speech in which he had mentioned the treaty and Mr. Sumner personally, he said: "I felt very much tempted to say more about you than I did, but I know you shrink from ovations and public compliments, all of which, however, you cannot expect to escape. I did not say, as the telegraph (I am told) has it, that you were in favor of ratifying the St. Thomas treaty; but I said that you had done more than anybody else to save the treaty from an untimely death." Here is a testimony from the person who was most interested and best informed as to Mr. Sumner's course which assigns to him more effective aid than any given by any one, including Mr. Seward himself, "to save the treaty from an untimely death;" testimony directly in the teeth of Miss Seward's intimation of sinister silence, double dealing and suppression.

No other and contrary statements, it is presumed, were ever made by him ; for if made, they would show him to be other than the honest and truthful man he was believed to be. The General, as still further showing his absolute confidence in Mr. Sumner, bespoke his friendly intervention in the embarrassed relations between Prussia and Denmark, and said : "I find to my great regret that we are not making any progress in our relations with Prussia; and I wish you would lend a hand in bringing about a really good understanding and sincere neighborly relations between us and the North German Confederacy. We (I mean my colleagues and myself) are anxious for it, but every time we make an overture or an approach we are repulsed in such a manner as to make it almost impossible with self-respect to make new attempts. . . . . I really know no other man in the world who could as well as you, being the friend of both, help us out of this unsatisfactory state of things, and thereby remove one of the existing causes of war." A European who could solicit in such terms the friendly intervention of an American citizen in the relations between his own and another kingdom must have held in remarkable confidence and esteem the foreigner to whom he applied.

Miss Seward deals disingenuously with this speech. She cites it as made in June, 1869, in the Rigsdag, whereas it was made May 13, at the banquet ; but exact time and place are unimportant, except as bearing on her method of dealing with facts. She quotes three sentences from the speech, and at the end of the first one there are stars, indicating an omission. The next sentence was the following, at which she was careful to stop. "It must, however," continued General Raasloff, "not be forgotten that the treaty has not been rejected ; its ratification has only been postponed, and that it is so is owing to the stand taken by some few wise statesmen, foremost among whom is my friend, the Hon.

Charles Sumner, one of the most prominent and experienced statesmen of the age, for many years the leader of the Senate in regard to foreign relations, and a man who never loses sight of the regard and consideration due from one friendly nation to another."

Miss Seward might well omit this sentence, as it spoils entirely her theory. The omission of Mr. Seward's name from the speech is significant. He had led the Danish negotiator into a pitfall, and his name therefore received no grateful mention. Raasloff's career as a public man ended with his diplomatic failure, and with the fall of his ministry as the consequence; and leaving his country he passed the rest of his life abroad, chiefly in Paris, and died in the suburb of Passy, February 14, 1883, at the age of sixty-seven. He was in New York in May, 1872, but he had become soured by disappointment, and kept aloof from Washington.

Within a month before General Raasloff left Washington in 1869, there was a new President, General Grant, and a new Secretary of State, Mr. Fish, neither of whom showed favor to the treaty, the former dismissing it summarily as "a scheme of Seward's and he would have nothing to do with it;" and the latter sending Mr. Sumner notes which indicated an adverse leaning. As appears by one bearing date October 8, 1869, Mr. Fish peremptorily refused, at the urgent request of De Bille, the new Danish minister, to ask for another extension of time for the ratification, leaving De Bille to ask for it, and took pains to guard against any expression in favor of its ratification. A few months later, January 28, 1870, he transmitted to Mr. Sumner, for use at his discretion, a letter from R. C. Kirk, Minister Resident at Buenos Ayres, dated December 13, 1869, who, in an account of a recent visit, described St. Thomas as "one of the most God-forsaken islands;" "the great majority of its inhabitants filthy-looking negroes," subject to earthquakes, one of which occurred on the morning of his arrival, and the island itself as "not desirable even as a gift."

Miss Seward undertakes to give matters of record concerning the treaty which at the time she wrote were under the seal of secrecy. But upon the removal of the injunction, January 5, 1888, on Mr. Hoar's motion, it was found that Mr. Sumner did not, as she states, indorse "the one word, 'adversely,' on the treaty," and that neither he nor any one indorsed that or any other words upon it, it being absolutely free from any notes whatever. Even the wrapper contains only a memorandum of the reference to the committee. The words "suspension of action" which she puts in quotation marks as Mr. Sumner's recommendation, are her words, not Mr. Sumner's or the committee's.

The committee took definite action at the time General Raasloff left Washington finally. It laid the treaty on the table March 30, 1869, and recorded on its minutes the words, "the understanding being that this was equivalent to rejection and was a gentler method of effecting it." For his sake it held back its report for a year, and then cleared its docket. By the official transcript from the record, it appears that on March 24, 1870, Mr. Sumner reported the treaty "with the recommendation that the Senate do not advise and consent to the ratification of the same," with a similar report on the proposed extension of time. Miss Seward's fidelity to facts will be understood on recurring to her article, where she says that "the matter was never brought before the Senate and may be said to have been smothered in committee!" The record, as now open to the public, it may be added, shows Mr. Sumner's faithful attention to the business in repeated motions for references of documents.

Of the Committee on Foreign Affairs to which the St. Thomas treaty was referred, Cameron[1] of Pennsylvania, Patterson of New Hampshire, and Harlan of Iowa, alone survive. Their testimony has been requested, and after a reading of Miss Seward's "Episode," is cordially given. It should be read in the light of her charges and insinuations of "smothering" and dishonorable reticence, and her assumption that the argument for the acquisition was so self-evident and conclusive that it became "morally impossible to report openly against it," and that neither the Committee nor any Senator "could assign a reason for an adverse report." This is not the first time that an advocate sorely pressed finds it easier to assume than to argue.

Mr. Cameron writes: "The rejection of the treaty was quite a simple matter; there was no mystery about it. No person on the Foreign Affairs Committee was in favor of the treaty. The case of Alaska was very different, in which one of the chief motives was to show our regard for Russia for the part she had taken during the war, and to strengthen the northwestern possessions. The St. Thomas purchase made no impression upon the committee or upon the public either. The smothered at-

[1] Mr. Cameron has since died.

tack upon Mr. Sumner in this [Miss Seward's] article is most unjust."

Mr. Patterson writes: "I have read the article by Miss Seward with a good deal of interest and more surprise. The Senate, generally, I believe, regarded the treaty for the purchase of St. John and St. Thomas about as General Grant did, as one of Seward's schemes, and determined to have nothing to do with it. Some denied the constitutionality and more rejected the policy of entering upon a system of annexing non-contiguous territory and outlying islands to the United States." He states that the vote of the islanders was regarded by senators as a mere farce, and that not being fit for self-government, how they were to be governed when annexed to a self-governing people was a problem not easily solved; that in time of war the island would have been the first object struck at by an enemy, and would have required for its defense a great increase of our military and naval force; and that the finishing stroke to the treaty, already meeting with no favor anywhere, was given by a contemporaneous earthquake and tidal wave. He adds: "The reason why the Senate did not act promptly on the treaty, but allowed it to die on its hands, was a desire, if possible, to save the liberal ministry of Denmark, which had been drawn into that measure, against the natural effect of its rejection."

Mr. Harlan in his letter concurs with his associates in the opinion that "as a mere commercial transaction the proposed purchase at the price named would have been a great folly;" that "as a naval depot and coaling station St. Thomas would be of doubtful value to the United States;" and "as it did not appear to the committee to be specially desirable as a military station, they decided unanimously, I think, not to recommend the ratification of the treaty." As to the charge of unjustifiable delay on the part of the committee he writes, "In this case the committee were not, I think, dilatory. Ample but only necessary time was taken to make the necessary investigations and inquiries, and for the interchange of views; and when they decided not to recommend the ratification it was thought that it would seem less harsh towards the other power to permit the time for exchanging ratifications to expire than to formally reject the proposed cession." In relation to the inquiry as to whether the chairman, Mr. Sumner, acted fairly in the transaction, Mr. Harlan adds, "None who ever knew Mr. Sumner could have any doubt on that point. He was the soul of candor and frankness. And if he had been disposed to act otherwise in the case referred to, he could not have trifled with the Senate Committee on Foreign Affairs as then constituted." It is perhaps worthy of observation that the Senate appears to have unanimously acquiesced in the views of the committee.

Such is the true version of the "diplomatic episode," or rather of the diplomatic fiasco, and a final question may be asked : If the acquisition of St. Thomas was so manifestly desirable as Miss Seward represents, how does it happen that no one at Washington or among the people during the twenty years since Mr. Seward left office has said a word to revive the scheme? A good thing does not die so easily. There will always be true men and wise men to appreciate what is of enduring value. We have since had six Presidents, Grant, Hayes, Garfield, Arthur, Cleveland and Harrison, and, not counting Washburne, five Secretaries of State, Fish, Evarts, Blaine, Frelinghuysen and Bayard ; but none of them has coveted this island of the Caribbean Sea, rifted by earthquakes, swept by cyclones, and submerged by tidal waves, the imagined centre of universal commerce and a necessary outpost for our national defense ! Journals and merchants have been alike silent. Foreign nations, who were suspected to be greedy spectators, have turned away from the prize. St. Thomas remains still a Danish spinster, as she has been for two hundred years, unwedded and unsought. One lone sigh over her continued isolation comes from the namesake of a statesman who saw visions of her fairness and her dowry hidden altogether from the eyes of his own and of this generation.

www.ingramcontent.com/pod-product-compliance
Lightning Source LLC
LaVergne TN
LVHW020631110826
845149LV00004B/1144

* 9 7 8 1 4 1 8 1 8 6 6 9 2 *